Original title:
Life, According to the Fortune Cookie

Copyright © 2025 Creative Arts Management OÜ
All rights reserved.

Author: Ethan Prescott
ISBN HARDBACK: 978-1-80566-087-3
ISBN PAPERBACK: 978-1-80566-382-9

The Unexpected Message

In a tiny shell, wisdom waits,
A crumb of fate on dinner plates.
Twist and crunch, surprise in hand,
Laughter sparks, as jokes expand.

'You will soon tie up your shoes,'
The universe plays tricks, it woos.
A shoe-snagged dance, a funny sight,
Stumbling charges through the night.

Tasty Tidings

Dinner ends with words so sweet,
A hidden joke in every treat.
'You will find joy in the most absurd,'
Like slipping on a cat, that's the word!

Chuckle now at just one bite,
Crumbs of wisdom, pure delight.
In every fortune, a plot twist lies,
Even small slips can lead to highs.

Slices of Serendipity

With every crunch, a story unfolds,
Messages wrapped in crispy folds.
'Your socks will vanish in the night,'
Now even laundry's got a bite!

Mystery meals with fortune's flair,
Loss and gain, keep them fair!
A tango of chance, a dance so grand,
With sweets of wisdom now in hand.

Crumbs of Destiny

A crack and a grin, what could it be?
'Your future holds a dance of glee!'
Shuffling through with two left feet,
Tripping on joy can't be beat!

'Fortune favors those who laugh,'
Giggling madly, take your path.
In every bite, a riddle's charm,
Keep smiling on, it's good luck's warm!

Whispers of Cracked Shells

In a tiny shell, wisdom sleeps,
Beneath the crunch, a secret peeks.
Don't take it serious, have some fun,
The best advice? Eat another bun.

Fortunes crack with every bite,
Telling tales of sheer delight.
If you trip while dancing today,
Just blame it on the noodles, hey!

Secrets in Sweet Fortunes

Cracked tastes reveal the simplest truths,
Like cats, or socks, or dancing youths.
Laughter echoes in every bite,
While dreams take wing like kites in flight.

A fortune said to count your ducks,
But honestly, who gives a clucks?
Spin the wheel of whims today,
And toast to crumbs that sailed away!

A Slice of Tomorrow

Open wide, the future peeks,
In sprinkles, giggles, and chicken leaks.
Tomorrow served on a silver plate,
With a side of joy, it's worth the wait.

Forks have answers, or so they say,
Just don't get lost along the way.
The pie's half gone, but who needs more?
We're all just crumbs on fortune's floor!

Charmed Predictions

Fortunes dance in sugar coats,
Swirling hints like drowsy goats.
Wear mismatched socks; it's a sign,
Tomorrow's disco will be divine!

A rabbit's foot and a noodle's twist,
In charming riddles, don't be missed.
Crispy words in every bite,
Fueling dreams through the starry night!

A Taste of Tomorrow

Tomorrow whispers sweet and sly,
While dinner's served with a hopeful eye.
Crunchy wisdom, take a bite,
Fortunes crumble, in the light.

Noodles twist, and laughter rolls,
Each message sneaks into our souls.
Ginger tea and giggles mix,
Tomorrow's tricks are all in the fix.

Wrapped in Serendipity

In a packet bright and cheery,
Promises dance with strokes quite eerie.
If you're lost, just check the tray,
Hilarity leads you on your way!

Unwrap the laughter, find the fate,
Chopsticks twirl, don't hesitate!
A twist of luck in every bite,
Wrap yourself in pure delight!

A Crunch of Know-How

Crunchy bits with wisdom's flair,
Each bite's a joke, if you dare.
When plans get sticky, take a chance,
Fortune cookies love to dance!

A nugget here, a giggle there,
Sprinkle joy on every layer.
When the chips are down, be bold,
Fortune's laughter never gets old!

Silken Threads of Fate

Silken threads weave tales so sly,
Peeking out from snacks nearby.
Follow the whispers, take a taste,
Fortune's light is never chaste.

A sprinkle of luck, a dash of spice,
Mix in your hopes, add some nice.
With every crunch, a laugh you'll find,
Threads of joy twist and unwind.

The Sweet Prologue

A slip of paper speaks to me,
With wisdom wrapped in mystery.
It says, don't sweat the small stuff,
Instead, just eat some tasty fluff.

A crinkle, crackle, and a grin,
Perhaps my fortune's made of tin!
But laughter spills like hot tea,
As I savor treats blissfully.

A Morsel of Tomorrow

Tomorrow holds a wild treat,
A message tucked in my sweet eat.
Cry not for plans that go amiss,
For every chaos brings a bliss.

With chopsticks poised, I take a bite,
Fortune cookies take to flight!
Shattering fears like glass so fine,
What's broken can become divine.

Secrets from the Edible

A clandestine message within each shell,
It tickles my heart, what the biscuits tell.
'Adventure awaits at the lunch hour!'
Savoring crumbs, I feel the power.

Should I trust this crispy sage?
It thinks I'm wise beyond my age!
With snacks in hand, I'll dare to roam,
For even silly dreams feel like home.

Charms of the Unknown

Peeking inside the crispy fold,
'You'll find great joy if you're bold!'
I chuckle while munching my prize,
Each bite reveals more strange surprise.

The universe in sesame seed,
Encouragement in a tiny deed.
Out of chaos, fun's often born,
In cookies, wisdom is never worn.

The Oracle in the Dessert

In a box so small, wisdom swings,
Crumbs of truth on golden wings.
Chocolate chips and almond paste,
Whispers of fate, oh what a taste!

Lemon tarts with playful jive,
Sweets reveal how we should strive.
The crumbs scatter, some align,
A sprinkle of humor, oh so fine!

Insights from Starlit Bites

From crispy shells, the secrets flow,
Like shooting stars that put on a show.
Fortunes twist, they giggle and dance,
In a bite-size that's more than chance.

Peanut butter and jelly dreams,
Coconut flake, or so it seems.
Count your blessings, skip your dues,
Laughter waits in every choose.

Hidden Truths Beneath the Crunch

In crispy wraps of pure delight,
Lurk funny truths like stars at night.
A secret here, a giggle there,
Unwrap the laughs, with tasty flair.

Crack them open, see what's next,
A fortune that leaves all perplexed.
Run faster, take the leap today,
The only way to live, they say!

Messages in a Crunchy Wrap

Wrapped so tight, the secrets hum,
With laughter bold, and feeling dumb.
Open wide and take a chance,
In every crunch, there's room to dance.

Twisted tales of fate and fun,
In every bite, a riddle spun.
The answers hide in salty glaze,
Find them quick, let humor blaze!

A Bite of Destiny

In one small crunch, truth unfurls,
A hint of humor in this world.
Crack it open, hear the chime,
It'll suggest you dance on a dime.

Your future's bright, the cookie said,
But now there's crumbs in your bed.
Coins will come, or so it hints,
Just don't borrow from the mints.

Seek balance, it supports our goals,
Like sauces fighting over bowls.
Need to giggle, take a look,
The answers hide in every nook.

So nibble slow, don't rush the snack,
Find wisdom while you munch and crack.
Your fate's a laugh, a sprinkle of fun,
Let frolic and crunch come, one by one.

Secrets from a Snack

In tiny bites, the truths appear,
With silly wisdom, have no fear.
The crispy shell holds laughs galore,
One fortune reads, 'Look for more!'

Drop the fuss, and wear a grin,
The cookie's magic lies within.
A sprinkle of joy, a dash of zest,
Here's a tip: just be your best!

Dare to ask for extra rice,
For fortune favors being nice.
Who knew courage came in sprinkles,
Or humor lived in crunchy crinkles?

Find a fortune, share it loud,
A twist of fate to make you proud.
These snacks of wisdom, oh so spry,
Can turn a tear into a fry!

Tiny Wisdoms Encased

In wrappers crinkled, secrets hide,
With each small nibble, joy applied.
Expect a dance, a snort, a cheer,
Messages that tickle, oh so dear!

"The road less traveled needs good shoes,"
Said one that followed a pumpkin muse.
"Your soulmate's waiting at the booth,"
Don't look! Just laugh; it's only truth.

Bite a chunk, let giggles bloom,
Sprouting fun in every room.
Remember: work hard, eat dessert,
And don't forget to wear a skirt!

The cookie says you'll shine so bright,
Even wearing socks that don't fit right.
Conversations spin in silly tones,
When crackling bites become your own.

Messages in the Moonlight

Under stars, a fortune glows,
A night of laughs, that's how it goes.
"Kick back! Your worries are quite absurd,"
Said one that's been thoroughly stirred.

"Find a dance partner who owns a cat,"
That wisdom surely made me splat.
For life is fun, just take a hint,
With every crunch, a cheerful glint.

Steal a moment, break the mold,
The cookie's love is pure and bold.
"Ice cream first, then the soup,"
Oh, foolish hearts! Let's form a troop!

A laughter shared beneath the sky,
Makes every moment seem to fly.
In cookie crumbs, let friendship nest,
The funniest tales, you'll know the best!

Cracked Insights

In a paper shell, truths unfold,
A munch of fate, both hot and cold.
The wisdom stirs, but who can tell,
If fortune smiles or casts a spell?

With every crunch, a giggle grows,
Tales of riches, ups and lows.
Who knew the cookie held the key?
To all the mysteries of my spree!

A nibble here, a slip of fate,
With sprinkles of luck that simply await.
But still I ponder, chart my course,
Will I find joy, or just remorse?

So here's to crumbs, and sweet delight,
With laughs that sparkle, oh what a sight!
For every fortune that I read,
I'll munch my way through every need!

The Enigma of Flavor

Wrapped in paper, a tasty quest,
Each bite's a puzzle, not like the rest.
What does it mean? A giggle or sigh?
A twist of fate with a sprinkle of pie!

Flavors collide, in chaos they blend,
With every crunch, do messages send?
Will my next meal be one of the best?
Or am I doomed to eternal jest?

Under sweet layers, wisdom creeps,
A sage's joke while the doughnut sleeps.
Let's feast on mysteries that twist our fate,
As every fortune leads me to wait.

A scoop of humor, a dash of spice,
Open the box, oh what a slice!
With every morsel, new thoughts arise,
In the crusty shells, laughter lies!

Sweets and Secrets

Crunch and munch, the secrets hide,
In folded dreams where fortunes bide.
What's next for me, a jackpot or fall?
Or maybe a dance with a cat at the mall?

A sprinkle of luck on a plate of fate,
Confetti dreams that resonate.
Laughter rings out with each wise crack,
As I chase my whims, there's no turning back!

With sugary spritz and a side of cheer,
Every nibble whispers, 'Don't you fear.'
For life's a treat, a candy parade,
Where jokes are the best fortune ever made!

So raise a toast to sweetened views,
With flavors that swap like playful clues.
In every crunch, the truth is a quirk,
Let's munch our way through life's silly work!

Echoes of the Unknown

In fortune's grip, perceptions switch,
Every bite reveals a quirky pitch.
Will I fall in love, or just in soup?
Mysteries swirl in a crunching loop!

Crumbs of wisdom scatter around,
As giggles bubble, knowledge found.
With each chomp, the laughter flows,
Could the cookie run the world's shows?

A hint of fate in every taste,
Most journeys start with a sweet little waste.
So munch and ponder as you go,
With wisdom funnier than we know!

Through crispy truths and glazed delight,
Let's toast the echoes that take flight.
For every fortune in a bite,
Leads us on a merry, silly flight!

The Hidden Message

In a tiny shell, wisdom's hidden,
Cracking jokes, like a show that's bidden.
Fortunes scribbled in crumbs of delight,
Who knew snacks could predict our plight?

Eat with glee, and watch your fate,
A laugh awaits, don't hesitate.
The wisdom's simple, the truths absurd,
Adventures await; just say the word!

Secrets from the Shell

Twist and crack, a crunch so loud,
Hidden secrets beneath the crowd.
Chinese whispers in a crispy fold,
Eat quick, before they turn cold!

Don't take it all too seriously,
Dreams come true, but be curious!
Pop that shell, let laughter soar,
What's next? Who knows, but you'll want more!

Prophecies in a Crisp Wrapper

Wrapped up tight in a golden layer,
Promises made by a crispy player.
Each bite holds a twist of fate,
Or advice on when to take a break!

The future's scribbled in funky text,
"Make a cat your next close friend," it suggests.
Take it lightly, enjoy the ride,
With a cookie's wisdom as your guide!

Sweet Nothings Revealed

In sugary whispers, fortunes unfold,
Sweet nothings, stories told.
Chuckle at truths wrapped in delight,
Each munch brings giggles in the night!

Crack open joy, share a grin,
With every bite, let the laughs begin.
Life's a jest, or so they say,
Make the most of it, come what may!

Tantalizing Tidings

A crack and a snap, the fortunes unfold,
Surprises await, both funny and bold.
If you trip over luck, don't fear a fall,
Just laugh at the fate served up in a brawl.

A cookie in hand, a giggle escapes,
You're destined for something, like cupcakes with grapes.

For every sweet crunch, a wacky delight,
Turn any dull day into a fabulous night.

So heed all the messages, large and small,
They may not be clear, but they're quirky for all.
If the secret is simple, just roll with the cue,
And claim that the universe's in on the joke too.

Your future's a canvas, a whimsical scene,
Paint it with laughter, keep it fresh and clean.
For who needs a map or a careful GPS,
When munching on cookies can lead to success?

The Sweet Whisper

A little chip whisper, with frosting in tow,
Promises galore, like sprinkles in dough.
Glimmers of wisdom, not so sage or deep,
But giggles for days, oh, how they can keep!

Chasing rainbows made of chocolate and cream,
Fortunes that tease, like a whimsical dream.
Unlocking the joy, with each cracked veneer,
Every nibble taken becomes a cheerleader.

So grab that crisp fortune, don't let it resell,
Embrace the absurd, in this cookie shell.
You might find your answer, wrapped in a joke,
Or at least some new wisdom, from the crumbs it broke.

When dough meets delight, and laughter takes flight,
The world spins around, in a whirl of bright light.
So savor each moment, and don't take a pause,
For life's a sweet fortune, with edible laws!

Glimpses Hidden in the Treat

Bite into the mystery, nibble the charm,
Each crunchy layer brings a smile, no harm.
What lurks in the shadows, a jest or jab?
Fries lost in fortune, a whimsical crab!

The kernel of wisdom, wrapped in a dough,
Surprises unravel, with flavors that flow.
Tickles and laughs tucked in each crumbed fold,
Decoding the giggles, a treasure untold.

Perhaps it's a dance, or a flick of a glance,
A chance to be silly, to leap and to prance.
Ode to the fortune, that's almost too mad,
To read with a frown would be utterly bad!

So gather your friends, and share the delight,
For luck's in the laughter that shines so bright.
In each little treat, let humor rule supreme,
Embrace the goofy, make it your theme!

The Epiphany Crunch

A crunch from the cookie, a giggle it brings,
Like wisdom from kittens in butterfly wings.
Flavors of fortune, a zesty review,
Caught in the web of what cookies can do.

Pick a crumb, make a wish, let the fun start,
Giddy as raindrops dance, joy fills your heart.
What's next on the docket? A pizza-shaped cat?
Oh, all that's missing is a noodle-top hat!

Insights are wacky, in shimmering forms,
Like thoughts you'd expect from whimsical storms.
Just shake off the heavy, let silly prevail,
Each bite's an adventure, through laughter you sail.

So raise up your cookies, with laughter and cheer,
For moments of joy are what we hold dear.
In a world of pretzels, let cookies be great,
Crunch wisdom with laughter—why hesitate?

The Tantalizing Enigma

Inside a shell, wisdom hides,
A cryptic giggle it provides.
The future's bright, but watch your step,
For fortune cookies, do misrep!

A slip of paper brings a grin,
But will it lead to loss or win?
'A spoonful of sugar' took me far,
Now I'm searching for my car!

Eat with glee, discard the fear,
Your next adventure's near, my dear.
Each crunch a riddle, tasty tease,
Just don't forget to say "please!"

So laugh and munch, but heed the sign,
A strange fate may be close behind.
Fortune cookies, sly and bold,
Their secrets never truly told!

Prescriptions from the Crisp

Doctors say just eat more luck,
A cookie a day keeps you in luck.
Crunch your worries, munch your woes,
Prescriptions wrapped in paper flows!

'Go for a run', it boldly states,
It knows my couch, it knows my rates.
But what if I choose to just stay snug?
I'll take my fortune in a mug!

The crunching sound brings hope anew,
What shall I eat? A bowl or two?
Glimpses of glory, crumbs of fate,
Munch away while you still wait!

These whims and wishes, all in fun,
Not meant to stress or make you run.
So take a bite and let it flow,
And trust the cookie knows what's so!

Unfolding Myths

Cracks upon the wrapper divide,
A fortune shines, can't run, can't hide.
'You'll travel far', it makes me laugh,
Right to the fridge? I'll take half!

This tiny scroll rolls out the spout,
Mysteries of what's in and out.
'You'll meet someone', oh what a twist,
Was it that pizza I almost missed?

So much wisdom in small bites,
A squeak, a chuckle, late-night fights.
Open your heart to the unknown,
Truth or myth, all can be shown.

A fortune rolls into my maze,
On this snack, my worries blaze.
A crispy crunch with tales to weave,
Who knew these cookies could deceive!

A Coded Snack

A kernel of truth in every crunch,
Decoding fortunes during lunch.
'Your ship has come', it slyly claims,
But I just want snacks, stop playing games!

Around the table, whispers swirl,
The fortune's fate begins to twirl.
'You'll shine bright', it says with glee,
But first, excuse the crumbs—oh me!

Messages hidden, sweet delight,
Unravel mysteries, hearts take flight.
'Beware of strangers', a warning read,
Was it about the mouse, or about bread?

These tasty notes, they make me grin,
No need for boxes; let's dig in!
So grab a cookie, take a chance,
In this coded snack, we laugh and dance!

Dice of Destiny

In the roll of chance, we find our plays,
Eight-legged noodle runs on purple days.
Fortune smiles with a twinkle and wink,
Let's gamble our woes, pour another drink.

Peeking through paper, a fortune awaits,
"Dance with the pigeons, avoid heavy weights."
With chopsticks in hand, we stir up the fun,
Who knew that mischief could weigh a ton?

Laughter erupts with each thrilling bite,
Lost in the sauce, it feels just right.
A twist of the wrist, a flick of the bean,
Fate's a surprise wrapped in fried cuisine.

Unraveled Mystique

Beneath the crunch, secrets lay bare,
Whispers of wisdom tucked strange as a pair.
"Watch for the owls, they speak in rhymes,"
I chuckle while dreaming of spaghetti times.

On a paper slip, in fancy typeface,
"Find treasure in socks, it's a magical place!"
I scour my drawer, with a hopeful glance,
While mismatched footsies lead me to chance.

In momentous bites, the world spins around,
Noodles dangle high as fortune unwound.
Dreams on the table, all tangled and neat,
Mirth on the menu, with every treat.

Threads of Tomorrow

Stitches of stories weave through the day,
Fortune cookie giggles, come what may.
"Wear two different shoes, and dance in the rain,"
I'm prancing away, free from the mundane.

The future's a riddle spun tight with a thread,
Wrap it in laughter, watch worries spread.
"Pick dandelions, they'll brighten your frown,"
A bouquet of wishes, let's twirl in the town.

In yesterday's batter, tomorrow takes flight,
Silly confessions in the dimming light.
Each bite a tangle, of fate we create,
Let's stitch up our dreams and decorate!

Glazed Insights

Sugary whispers from a shell so bright,
Sticky with mischief that shines in the night.
"Join the circus, juggle your fears,"
Unraveled delights bring giggles, not tears.

From buttery fortune, the truth is revealed,
"Bake cookies, but don't forget to shield!"
I flour my face, caught in a sweet mess,
Each crumb tells a joke, I couldn't have guessed.

As sprinkles fall like stars from above,
Life's a wild dance; let's trip, let's love.
With donuts of dreams and muffins of cheer,
Sweetest of fortunes, let's shimmy and steer!

Enchanted Anticipations

A tiny slip, wrapped with fate,
Promising joy, but through the gate.
Read it quick, before it's gone,
What should I wear? A tux, or a fawn?

Mystic crumbs, for those who dare,
Do I get rich? Or just a hair?
It says to dance like no one minds,
Guess I'll leap, but trip on blinds!

Nuggets of Fortune

Crunchy bites of wisdom sweet,
Says I'm charming, can't be beat.
Tomorrow's meal is set to munch,
But should I wear my grass-stained crunch?

Cookies crack, and laughter stirs,
With each bite, absurdity blurs.
A future bright? Or just a tease?
Maybe my hair will grow with ease!

Morsels of Tomorrow

Chips of fate in a crinkly wrap,
Forecasting bliss with a silly map.
It whispers dreams of endless fun,
With extra hugs when day is done.

A hint to run and chase the sun,
Or perhaps just snack till we weigh a ton?
Jokes and giggles, the fortune's flair,
I'll take that one, oh, what a pair!

Waves of Happenstance

Fortunes flow like a funky tide,
Washing worries to the side.
A gem of wisdom in this swell,
'Watch for ducks'—who can tell?

Crumbs of fate on a cereal bowl,
Combining dreams beyond control.
Dance on pancakes, glide on bread,
The future's funny when well-fed!

A Dash of Serendipity

In a world full of crumbs, we dance and we shuffle,
Munching on dreams while we giggle and guffaw.
With sprinkles of fortune and unexpected trouble,
    We spill all our secrets without even a flaw.

    Laughter spills out from these crinkly slips,
    As fortunes come wrapped in a sugary glaze.
    We bite on the whims, we taste with our tips,
        In the kitchen of life, we're all chefs of craze.

Curved Paths and Future Stars

Take the long road, it's winding and tight,
You'll meet a wise turtle selling socks for your feet.
He'll tell you a joke that will lighten your night,
In his shell of a shop, you'll find snacks to eat.

Stars twinkle like points on a chaotic map,
With each twist we take, a new surprise reveals.
We tumble and trip, but there's joy in the flap,
After all, who knew futures could come in wheels?

Fortune's Favor

Crack open that cookie, hear the crumble snap,
What did it say? Oh wait, was it a joke?
A treat for the tummy or a funny mishap?
Fortunes can giggle, not always invoke.

Maybe your ruler was just out of stock,
Measure success in slices, not dreary old stacks.
When fortune's a prank, take off that old clock,
Twelve o'clock is a laugh, laugh loudly—relax!

Predictions Served Warm

Fresh from the fryer, predictions align,
There's wisdom in crumbs, served up with a grin.
Sugar-coated whispers, oh how they shine,
My future's a banquet; let's dig right in!

Saucy and sassy, with a twist on the side,
Each fortune unfolds like a well-cooked joke.
I'm savoring fate, with laughter as my guide,
At this feast of the unknown, I'll never feel broke.

Crunching Through Possibilities

In the wrapper of secrets, I take a bite,
A new adventure, what feels just right.
Pick a number, roll the dice,
Tomorrow might be cold, or super nice.

Each crunch unveils a brand new fate,
With each message, I eagerly await.
Will I dance with my dog in the rain?
Or find a million dollars by the train?

The cookie whispers, "Don't hesitate,"
A leap of faith tempts me, it's never too late.
But what if the truth is a big old prank?
I'll still consider it, thanks to that blank.

I'll take a gamble, reach for the sky,
Laugh at the fortunes, oh me, oh my.
So here's to the snacks that tell my tale,
In this silly game, I'll never fail!

Silent Signals

Crunch! The sound speaks louder than words,
Hidden meanings, like flocks of birds.
A twist, a turn, a joke on the side,
In every crunch I feel the joy coincide.

Fortunes come wrapped tight in a shell,
Tales of grandeur, or just plain swell.
Will I meet a cat with a top hat and cane?
Or find hidden treasure beneath the rain?

I ponder the future, sipping my tea,
Puns and riddles, oh what can they be?
A nudge from the universe, or just for fun?
With fortunes as wacky, I know I've won!

So here's to the signals, silent and clear,
I'll laugh at the mysteries, shed every fear.
In the grand scheme, it's just a charade,
With cookies and giggles, a silly parade!

Serene Predictions

In a world so calm, the cookie unfolds,
Tales of adventure and secrets untold.
Will I find a llama on my morning jog?
Or win a dance-off against a big dog?

Crispy wisdom from doughy delight,
Whispers of humor in the soft, moonlight.
An umbrella of stars decorating my dreams,
What's life without laughter? It's not what it seems.

With predictions serene, I take a deep breath,
Each crumb a promise, defying all death.
The trickster inside, playing games with glee,
Who knew an oasis could be so silly?

So I bite and I chuckle, predicting my fate,
Snacking on wisdom; it's never too late.
With cookies as guides, I will surely thrive,
In a quirky world where giggles arrive!

The Fortune Teller's Snack

A snack of divination, sweet and bold,
What mysteries await, what stories unfold?
Will I trip over rainbows on my way to the mall?
Or dodge a big puddle; I might just fall!

Each crunch a riddle, each bite a chance,
Dancing in flavors, a light-hearted dance.
Will a squirrel in a tuxedo stop and say, "Hi?"
Or will I end up in a pancake pie?

So munching on crumbs, I ponder it all,
Silly predictions that dance on my wall.
If laughter is magic, then I've struck gold,
With cookies as prophets, I'm brave and bold!

Fortunes you share, like candy from the sky,
With a giggle and crunch, let's give it a try.
The fortune teller's snack, what a tasty delight,
Bringing joy and chuckles, morning to night!

The Confectioner's Predictions

Inside this shell, a surprise awaits,
Future's wrapped in sugary states.
Bite down gently, let laughter unfold,
Tales of the whimsical, bright, and bold.

An ancient oracle, sweetly absurd,
With words that are silly, yet never blurred.
"Do not eat yellow snow," it seems to say,
And humor erupts with a nod and a sway.

Crumbs of wisdom, all sprinkled with glee,
"Dance like a chicken; it's good for thee."
Nonsense that tickles and makes the heart race,
These tasty nuggets just add to the chase.

Flavorful Forecasts

Tiny scrolls wrapped in crispy delight,
Offer up fortunes, all quirky and bright.
"You'll find a lost sock!" they cheekily say,
As you hop through the day in a whimsical way.

Gingerly opened, the laughter escapes,
With flavors of chaos, and prancing shapes.
"Beware of pigeons—they may steal your bread,"
Silly warnings that dance in your head.

The banquet of nonsense, served up on a plate,
Predictions so tasty, they're hard to hate.
Enjoy each morsel, get ready to grin,
For the wildest of journeys is about to begin.

Spiced Revelations

In a world where the bizarre is the norm,
These crispy slips offer a different form.
"Your socks are plotting a daring escape,"
Each bite brings laughter, no need for a tape.

With hints of cinnamon and a dash of nutmeg,
The fortune slips in like a well-placed keg.
"A llama will visit you soon at your door,"
Imagining layers of fun to explore.

Unraveling riddles in sugary dust,
A sprinkle of humor is always a must.
"Do cartwheels in public, embrace the absurd,"
The words serenade, their joy unreserved.

Crisp Edges of Tomorrow

Beneath the wrapper lies a whimsical thought,
Crisp edges teasing, a fortune is caught.
"Your cat knows secrets you're yet to unveil,"
This curious proclamation won't ever fail.

Witty predictions, like crunching sweet fries,
Each bite is a giggle, hilarity flies.
"Invest in mismatched socks, they'll rise to the top,"
Every morsel ensures that the fun's never stop.

The future is flaky and spiced just right,
With giggles and chuckles, and pure delight.
"Embrace the absurd!" the fortune does sing,
In this playful world, joy's always the king.

Cookies of Change

A cookie grinned with crumbs of fate,
It whispered secrets, don't be late.
Pick a fortune, take a bite,
Watch your day turn day to night.

It claims you'll win the lottery,
But first, you must find your key.
A little luck, a sprinkle of zest,
And a nap? Now that's the best!

What if it says a cat will stray?
How does it know? I ate it anyway!
A cookie's truth can twist and sway,
Hold on tight to what they say!

So here's a lesson from a baked delight,
Maybe charm your boss tonight.
If fortune's laughter fills your day,
Just feed it cookies; that's the way!

Beneath the Sugary Surface

Beneath the glaze, some words lie hid,
A fortune, it seems, is just a gig.
It might just say, 'You'll meet your match'
But also warns, 'Don't eat that hatch!'

Crack it open, let it reveal,
A mix of truths that seem surreal.
'Your luck will change,' it boldly proclaims,
While yours is stuck in quiet lanes.

With sprinkles of wit and bits of cheer,
A cookie's charm, oh dear, oh dear!
Who knew that crumbs could hold such weight?
Life's puzzles all wrapped up on a plate!

So grasp your cookie, don't feel shy,
A subject of laughter, oh my oh my!
For in its crack lies a funny tale—
Just remember not to inhale!

Whispers of the Riddle

In the hush of sweetness, secrets swirl,
A crispy riddle that makes one twirl.
It says, 'The best is yet to come!'
But what if it's just a cookie's hum?

Keep the fortune but share the dough,
A laugh is sweeter when shared, you know.
If today seems tough, seek cookie calm,
There's humor in the flour, a life charm.

It says, 'Beware of dog today,'
But is it real? Or just a play?
I'll offer biscuits, maybe a snack,
To smooth the barks and ease the flack.

So if a cookie gives you pause,
Don't worry much about its cause.
Life's riddles can sometimes sneak,
Into laughter, and that's no fluke!

Crumbs of Wisdom

A cookie crumbles, wisdom shared,
With every bite, you're slightly prepared.
It says, 'Don't worry, have some fun,'
While crumbs scatter, and it's nearly done.

Today's misfortune could be a giggle,
Tomorrow's laughter might make you wiggle.
And when all else crumbles to the floor,
Keep some crumbs; they're worth much more.

'A path not taken may be quite nice,'
Unless it leads you to a bowl of rice.
Then follow your nose, wherever it goes,
For wisdom often lies in cookie prose.

So here's the deal from a crispy treat,
Life's quirks are messy; they're hard to beat.
With laughter and crumbs, you'll surely thrive,
Just take a bite and feel alive!

Journey of a Thousand Cookies

With each crisp snap, a tale to tell,
A trip within a bakery, sweet and swell.
Glimpse of fortune tucked in dough,
Chasing crumbs where laughter flows.

Fortunes say to eat more pies,
But my pants scream, 'No more fries!'
Crunchy secrets in the air,
Who knew wisdom would be so rare?

Bite down hard, what will it say?
Dance with fate in a wobbly sway.
Laughter echoes, info's askew,
Smiles bring joy like soup to stew.

Each busting cookie tells a joke,
While fortune's keeper wears a cloak.
Choose your snack with harmless cheer,
Who knew life's lessons would taste so dear?

Fate Within a Crispy Shell

Beneath this shell, a mystery's snug,
Will it predict gains or a bug?
Open wide, and let out a sigh,
Turns out my future's a slice of pie.

"Great wealth is near," the paper shouts,
But my wallet just silently pouts.
Fortunes that tease, tales that play,
Who knew my luck would go astray?

Strips of wisdom, sugary charms,
Tripping through life with tasty arms.
Cookie crumbs scatter the floor,
Fortune frying pan, what's in store?

Bit by bit, we munch and gawk,
What's that? A blushing fortune talks!
"Your neighbor's cat holds the key,"
But all I want is more cookies for me!

Predictable Wonders

Open the wrapper, unfold the fate,
Will it tell me to nurture, or to wait?
"Adventure awaits," it boldly screams,
While I'm busy counting my dreams.

It tells me I'm bright as a star,
Too bad I'm just sitting in my car.
Crispy insights peel like bark,
Maybe it's right about that park?

"Find a new hobby," it advises me,
But knitting's a challenge, don't you see?
Yet here I sit, with snack in hand,
Laughing at quotes so out of hand.

Another fortune, whimsical tease,
Wishing for fried rice with ease.
Giggling at wisdom so delightfully round,
Who thought such nuggets could be found?

Nibbles of Knowledge

A snack to nibble, a truth to learn,
Open me up, it's my turn!
Silly fortunes in every twist,
Parting wisdom we can't resist.

"Change is coming," says the crunch,
I hope it's not another bunch!
Watch out for surprises, hot and cold,
I'd prefer my cookies over gold.

Whispers of fate in crispy delight,
Glimpse the funny in plain sight.
"Today you will meet a butterfly,"
Too bad I'm allergic; I might cry!

With each morsel, we laugh and grieve,
Fortunes hidden that we perceive.
Life's little snacks with a punchline here,
Tickling our senses, spreading cheer.

Beneath the Paper Thin

Beneath the paper thin
Lies wisdom forged in dough,
Your future rests in a crunch,
But it's best with some chow.

A fortune draped in humor,
Says joy is just a crumb,
Open wide and take a bite,
Your fate could be a pun.

The messages are silly,
Tales of cats and moons,
Watch out for the cosmic cats,
They dance to funny tunes.

So when you crack it open,
And laughter fills the room,
Know that life is filled with jokes,
Just add a touch of gloom.

Enigmas at the Table

Gather round the table, friends,
Enigmas wrapped in dough,
Between each bite of savory,
Could be wisdom we don't know.

"Eighty-five is just a number,"
Said the baker with a grin,
"Eat more noodles, dodge the gloom,
Fortunes come with a spin."

Giggles echo through the night,
As we ponder what's to be,
One fortune says to hug a tree,
The next, "Eat more brie."

With each crack of crispy shell,
A riddle on our plate,
Laughter fills the quirky air,
Our future tastes just great.

Foresight in the Flavors

Foresight comes in flavors,
Sweet, sour, salty, bold,
Each bite brings a secret tale,
Just waiting to be told.

"Beware of cats who dance," it said,
In bright and funny text,
In the kitchen we all laughed,
What on earth comes next?

A fortune filled with giggles,
Tells me to wear a hat,
Dance in circles, sing out loud,
And never pet a cat.

So with noodles and some luck,
We savor every taste,
In this feast of prophecies,
No moment goes to waste.

Prophecies Beneath the Crunch

Underneath the crispy crust,
A prophecy await,
"Tap dance on your neighbor's roof,
And do it while you skate."

Laughter bounces off the walls,
As friends munch side by side,
Each fortune winks conspiratorially,
With secrets sprinkled wide.

"A cat will steal your sandwich,"
The paper quips with flair,
We giggle as we munch away,
With crumbs beyond compare.

So take a chance on chicken,
Order sides that make you cheer,
For in each tasty morsel,
Are giggles for the year.

The Treat's Revelation

A cookie cracks, a wisdom bites,
Inside its shell, the truth ignites.
Crumbs of laughter sprinkle around,
Fortunes tumble, fate is found.

Secret messages in sweet disguise,
Glimpses of fortune in crunchy lies.
Eat your treat, don't skip the crunch,
Remember, it's just a cookie brunch!

Threads of an Inner Compass

Open wide that crispy treat,
What twists await in your next fleet?
A thread of fortune starts to weave,
In silly ways, you shan't believe!

Each slip of paper, a guiding plan,
"Dance like a chicken!" is the scam.
Guided by crumbs, take silly strides,
In wobbly paths, your fate resides.

Hidden Signals

The cookie's whisper, a playful jest,
"Your cat may plot to be the best!"
Read the lines between the grins,
Hiding gems where laughter begins.

Signals flutter like a flag in the breeze,
"Take a nap! And eat more cheese!"
Mischief wrapped in shiny foil,
Embrace the odd; let giggles uncoil.

Laced with Destiny

A fortune cookie, a sly delight,
Crafted secrets that take flight.
Laced with giggles, sprinkled cheer,
Cards of destiny, hold them near.

What's next for you? A swim in cake!
Or ride a llama? Make no mistake!
With crispy shells and hopes, we play,
Fortunes guide us in a funny way!

Silent Voices from the Past

In a crumpled slip, wisdom lies,
With giggles of ghosts under starlit skies.
They whisper of luck in a sugary tone,
Regrets taste sweet, though mostly alone.

Secret advice wrapped in crunchy fate,
Eat the fortune, then try to relate.
Crispy success is what they all crave,
But chocolate chips drown the world we save.

Luck's a joke, it's all in the spin,
Life gives you sprinkles, toss them in.
A dance with fortune, a twisty jig,
Beneath the laughter, a fortune big.

As you munch on the crumbs, take heed,
Silent echoes start to plant a seed.
Wear oversized shoes, walk with a grin,
Remember to laugh and let the fun win.

Savory Sagas

A taste of wisdom in a crunchy shell,
Dipped in honey, oh what a swell!
It tells you to dance and not fear the fall,
As fortune cookie crumbs have a ball.

In kitchens bustling, with aromas bright,
A batch of dreams bubble to delight.
Keep your friends close and your snacks closer,
Fortune told by this culinary composer.

Laughter spills over like sauce on a bowl,
Every nibble's a quest, a savory goal.
Fates twist like pasta, all tangled and silly,
Savor the spice, it's life's luscious filly.

As flavors mix and stories unwind,
The sweetest of giggles are what you'll find.
Nibble on fortune, let your palate decide,
In the grand saga of snacks, take it in stride.

Twisted Nuggets of Truth

Tiny messages tucked in folds,
Using bread crumbs to tell what's bold.
Silly truths in the crunch of fate,
Upside-down fortunes make for a great plate.

Eat your worries like a crunchy snack,
With each bite, let laughter attack.
Twisted delights in every crease,
Unraveling secrets that never cease.

Silly sayings wrapped tight in dough,
Round and round, just follow the flow.
Truths that wiggle like worms in the dirt,
Joyfully hidden beneath crispy shirt.

So pry open the secrets, but don't forget,
In laughter's embrace, there's no regret.
With each golden shell, a giggle awaits,
In the circus of fortune, it's all first rates.

Hidden Paths Await

Between the bites of sugary dreams,
Hidden paths twist with giggly themes.
Each crumb a riddle, a snack for your soul,
Leading to laughter, that's the ultimate goal.

Dare to open what's wrapped so tight,
Seek out the silliness, embrace the delight.
With crumbs on your chin and joy in your heart,
Every tiny fortune's a lovely new start.

Syrupy tales drizzled like fate,
Follow the whims, don't hesitate.
Life's a banquet, share your treats,
In this playful world, everyone eats.

So wobble your way through fortune's array,
Smiling at mishaps, let worries decay.
Giggles like sprinkles cover your day,
In hidden paths, there's only fun play.

Prophecies on Paper Slips

In a tiny crack, wisdom lies,
A crunch, a munch, a sweet surprise.
"You will find joy in a noodle bowl,"
As fortune slips from the sesame roll.

One night a cat will steal your chair,
But fortune smiles, if you just share.
"Beware of socks, they're tricky today,"
As if laundry holds secrets to sway.

A message wrapped in sweet delight,
"Take a nap, it feels just right!"
Your future glimmers in soy sauce drips,
From these prophesies on crispy strips.

When stress is thick as rice in stew,
Just open a cookie, and here's your cue:
"Dance like no one's watching, it's key,"
To happiness found in absurdity.

Fates Folded with Care

Folded fates in crispy form,
Whispers of mischief, breaking the norm.
"Your houseplants will thrive in the sun,"
Yet they wilted faster than I could run.

Small parchment dreams tucked in with flair,
"Adopt a goldfish, show it you care!"
As if swimming life lessons are neat,
In bubbles, they giggle, a charming feat.

"Try not to sip soup with your nose,"
Advising me like everyone knows.
Each slip of paper a giggle spree,
In this whimsical journey, come laugh with me.

Laughing fortunes tucked so tight,
Predicting antics in the moonlight.
"The dog may bark, but he means no harm,"
Just keep the treats, that's your best charm.

Sugar-Coated Epiphanies

In a sugar shell, confessions bloom,
Each crispy split a quirky loom.
"The fork will fall, but don't you fret,"
It's just a dance—get ready, bet.

Sweet little tidbits wrapped so tight,
"Your luck will change at half-past night!"
As if clocks know when fun is due,
Chasing the cat might just make two.

"You'll find answers in the fridge today,"
When all that's left is leftover play.
Oh, what wisdom in snacks and dips,
Inside each cookie, a joke that flips.

Slice of humor, sprinkled with glee,
Making wisdom a giggling spree.
"Your magic lies in chili spice,"
Bite after bite, take my advice.

Wisdom Wrapped in Wafers

Crisp wafers whisper, secrets to know,
"Don't wear a hat on a windy show!"
Before the wind plays its wild game,
Best to giggle and avoid the shame.

Dipped in chocolate, mischief awaits,
"Beware of mailmen, they steal your mates!"
A folding chaos, all in good fun,
Living in dreams where we laugh and run.

"Step on a crack, break your own back,"
Yet here I am, never looking back.
Cute proverbs bundled with sugary cheer,
Unwrap laughter; the end is quite near.

With each tasty bite, wisdom appears,
"Sing in the shower, ignore all your fears!"
Delightfully silly, each telling unfolds,
In laughter, dear friend, the universe holds.

Twists of Fate

In a box of secrets, I unseal,
A whisper of fortune, almost surreal.
Duck for cover when luck starts to sway,
Waffles and tears on an aimless buffet.

A cat on a roof sings a peculiar tune,
As if chasing dreams, under a sliver moon.
If laughter be gold, then I'm rich beyond scale,
But watch out for woes that tip-toe like snails.

Fortune's a jester, with hand-stitched attire,
Dancing on tables while we sit by the fire.
So raise up a glass to absurdity's art,
And learn how to chuckle at fate's wicked part.

With socks mismatched, and shoes untied,
I strut through the world, let chaos be my guide.
A fortune says, "Cheer up, just take a bite,"
Of dessert divine, which makes everything right.

Echoes of the Bamboo Grove

Crisp paper rustles, secrets untold,
Whispers of bamboo, colliding with bold.
A sage of the garden, with hair full of dew,
Says, "Forget about the past; it never had a clue."

With teacups clinking, fate's brew often spills,
Oh, how it tickles, then quietly thrills!
Jokes wrapped in wisdom exchanged every hour,
Even bamboo chuckles, "What's hard may empower."

There's fortune in waiting, a dance on a whim,
Like squirrels who ponder the size of a limb.
Chase maybes and what-ifs as shadows take flight,
And maybe a giggle will brighten up night.

Under moonlit laughter, we toast to the strange,
For life has its quirks, and fortunes rearrange.
So roll the dice, twist, and take a wild plunge,
In laughter's embrace, let mischief now lunge.

Unfolding Hope

A tiny scrap whispers, "Do not fret so!"
As fortunes tumble like marbles aglow.
Starfish on beach sigh of salt in the air,
While ice cream dreams melt without a care.

Mice wearing glasses, in suits they comply,
Debating the meaning of jellybean pie.
"You'll find your true purpose, it's hiding right there!"
Just behind that plant, with a dash of flair.

With crayons of chaos, I doodle my path,
Exploring the giggles that hide in the math.
Each curve of my journey may twist or ascend,
But draw out a smile, it's time to transcend.

So here's to the future, that delicate dance,
Like tiptoeing kittens who just need a chance.
Wrap hope in confetti and glitter so fine,
For every new stumble is just part of the line.

Sugared Predictions

With a crunch and a snap, the cookie gave in,
Dropping sweet stories wrapped thick with a grin.
A sprinkle of sugar, a pinch of the odd,
"Expect the unexpected," it winked, a façade.

Butterflies dance in the syrupy mist,
While fish hold their breath, as if something's amiss.
"Your future is tasty, just lend it an ear,"
Was it from the fortune or just from the beer?

A parade of oddities marches on by,
Starring in dreams as the seconds all fly.
"Time to take chances," the cookie implores,
While squirrels plan heists to raid distant stores.

So bathe in this chaos with glee and delight,
Sugar-coated futures are sparkly and bright.
For laughter's the frosting that sweetens the stars,
With fortunes so silly, we'll dance on guitars.

Glossy Hints of What's Next

Tiny slips hold truths so grand,
A crumpled message tucked in hand.
Eat more broccoli, it brightly states,
Yet here I am with all my plates.

A winding road with paths so strange,
Twists and turns and sudden change.
Dance like squirrels, the message laughs,
As I juggle my grocery drafts.

Laughter sparks in every bite,
Biting secrets, pure delight.
Next week claims I'll win it all,
Too bad my last bet was a stall.

So here's to fate, a kooky friend,
A sweetened kiss, a crazy trend.
With every crunch, a giggle blooms,
What awaits? Oh, who assumes?

The Gourmet Divination

Crack the shell, what do you find?
Fortunes wrapped in noodle twine.
Dine on wisdom, spice, and cheer,
Just don't choke; it's still unclear!

"Seek fortune on Tuesday!" it says,
Which Tuesday? I'm in quite a mess!
Eat dessert first, let worries slide,
But my cake's now a tsunami tide.

Chopsticks dance in a wobbly art,
While egg rolls bring some juicy heart.
"Adventure awaits! Take a leap!"
As I attempt to make a sweep.

For the secret sauce reveals in time,
That laughter's the best, without a dime.
So navigate each tasty bite,
With a grin that shines so bright!

Snippets of Fate

A crisp little note from a cookie's shell,
"Hold your horses!" or "Do quite well!"
But first, let's find some dipping sauce,
With a side of giggles, of course!

Wear stripes on Mondays and polka dots Tuesday,
Sandwich your blues, in a funny way.
Fortune finds me through mustard and glee,
What's cooking next? Who knows? Not me!

Charm your way through the noodle maze,
With peanut sauce to brighten days.
Chasing crumbs from the fortune of fries,
I wonder who writes these quirky lies!

A dash of thyme, a sprinkle of fun,
Laughter bubbles when all is done.
Secrets tucked in a doughy wrap,
Just remember, next time, take a nap!

The Oracle's Bite

What's in this crunchy little fold?
An oracle's secret, brave and bold!
"Bite into joy, but chew with care!"
While your dog eyes you with a stare.

Fortunes twirl like a spicy dance,
"Travel far and take a chance!"
But my couch calls louder than fate,
This week's adventure? A snack plate.

From almonds to noodles, all wrapped tight,
A message whispers, "Chase the light!"
But the fridge has a fabulous glow,
As I ponder what's next from the dough.

So grab your fortune, give it a whirl,
In the kitchen, let laughter unfurl.
Each cookie bite a giggling flash,
What's next? More snacks! A cookie stash!

www.ingramcontent.com/pod-product-compliance
Lightning Source LLC
Chambersburg PA
CBHW051631160426
43209CB00004B/597